MW01177964

MY FIRST LOOK
AT WEATHER

Earth gets heat from the sun

Heat

Maria Hidalgo

Creative Education

Published by Creative Education

123 South Broad Street, Mankato, Minnesota 56001

Creative Education is an imprint of The Creative Company

Designed by Rita Marshall

Photographs by CLEO Photography, Getty Images (Michael Dunning, Eitan Simanor, Konrad Wothe), JLM Visuals (Richard P. Jacobs, John Minnich), Tom Myers, James P. Rowan, Tom Stack & Associates (J. Lotter, Dr. Scott Norquay, Brian Parker, Bob Pool, Inga Spence, Mark A. Stack, Ryan C. Taylor, Greg Vaughan, Dave Watts)

Printed in the United States of America

Library of Congress Cataloging-in-Publication Data

Hidalgo, Maria. Heat / by Maria Hidalgo.

p. cm. — (My first look at weather)

Includes bibliographical references.

ISBN-13 : 978-1-58341-449-1

1. Heat—Juvenile literature. 2. Temperature—Juvenile literature. I. Title. II. Series.

QC256.H53 2006 536—dc22 2005037810

First edition 9 8 7 6 5 4 3 2 1

Heat

Feel the Heat

In the summer, you feel heat from the sun. In the winter, you warm up when you go inside or put on a coat. A **thermometer** can tell you exactly how hot or cold it is outside.

Even in the middle of winter, the sun helps to keep our planet warm. But you can make your own heat, too. Rub your hands together quickly as hard as you can. Your hands will feel warmer!

Even cold places get some sun and heat

The Sun and Heat

Different seasons have different **temperatures**. Spring and summer are usually warmer than fall and winter. That is because of the distance between Earth and the sun. The closer Earth is to the sun, the warmer it is.

Earth tilts as it turns. When one half of our planet is tilted toward the sun, that half of Earth has spring and summer. The other half

Heat from the sun helps make all weather happen, from a gentle breeze to a rainstorm.

THE SUN'S HEAT HELPS MANY PLANTS GROW

has fall and winter. Slowly, Earth tilts in the other direction, and different seasons begin.

The area around the middle of Earth is called the equator (*ee-KWAY-ter*). The temperature at the equator does not change much. The distance from the sun there is almost always the same.

Africa is a hot place. It can be 136 °F (57.8 °C) in the shade there. That is almost hot enough to fry eggs!

MOUNTAINS IN AFRICA ARE HOT AND DRY

Warm Wind, Cool Breezes

When air warms up, it rises. When the sun warms land, the air near the land warms up too. As this warm air rises, cooler air moves in to take its place. This is what causes wind. The wind you feel today might have started at the equator!

Hot-air balloons fly because they are filled with warm air, and warm air rises.

HOT-AIR BALLOONS ARE PUSHED BY THE WIND

It is often windy by oceans or lakes. Land heats up faster than water. Cooler air from over the water scoots in quickly as warm air rises off of the land. This makes wind.

Too Much Heat

We need heat from the sun to help plants grow and keep us warm. But too much heat is bad for Earth. Every time people make **pollution**, they change the air that is all around our planet.

Big cities can make lots of pollution

Pollution in the air acts like a blanket around Earth. Scientists are worried that this is heating up Earth too much. If the **glaciers** melt, our oceans might have too much water in them. And dry parts of Earth might not have enough water.

When the weather is hot

for a long time with no rain,

it is called a drought.

DROUGHTS CAN MAKE THE LAND LOOK CRACKED

Too much heat could make oceans too full

The sun is about 93 million miles (150 million km) from Earth. But it is close enough to give us all the heat we need. The next time you feel a warm breeze or sunlight, think about how important heat is to our weather and our lives!

The sun makes life on Earth possible

Hands-on: Make a thermometer

The liquid in a thermometer moves up when it is warm and down when it is cool. Try making your own!

What You Need

Water with food coloring in it

A clear straw

Soft clay

A glass of hot water

What You Do

1. Carefully pour a drop of the colored liquid into the clear straw.
2. Tap the straw until the drop is halfway down. Use the clay to plug the bottom of the straw.
3. Stand the straw in the hot water.

As air under the colored liquid heats up and expands, it will push the liquid up!

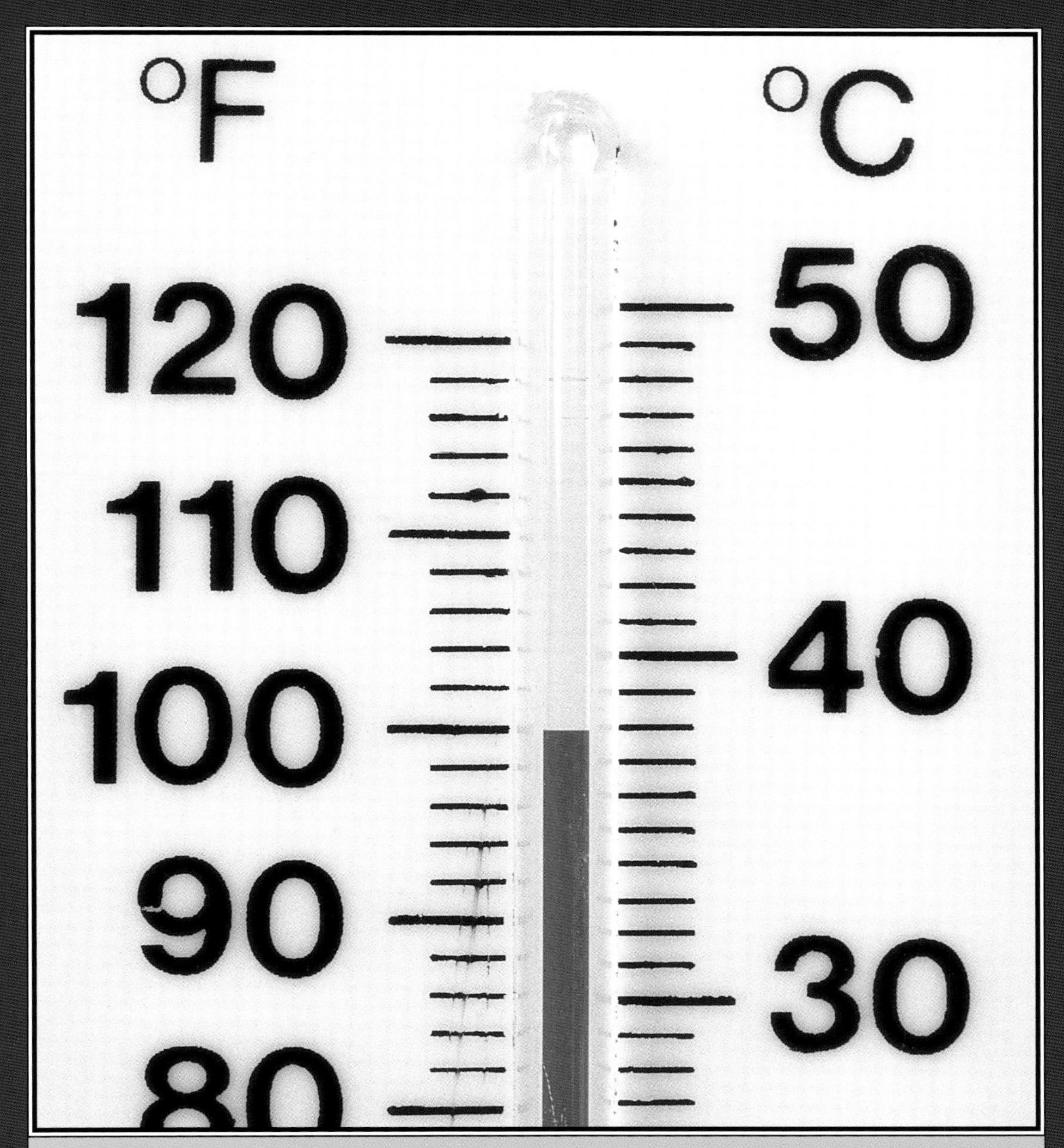

A THERMOMETER MEASURES HOW HOT THINGS ARE

Index

Words to Know

glaciers—huge areas of ice that last all year in cold parts of the world

pollution—smoke, garbage, or anything that makes the land, water, or air dirty

temperatures—exactly how hot or cold something is

thermometer—a special tube used to measure how hot or cold something is

Read More

Fandel, Jennifer. *Weather: Heat*. Mankato, Minn.: Smart Apple Media, 2002.

Mack, Lorrie. *Eye Wonder: Weather*. New York: Dorling Kindersley Limited, 2004.

Thomas, Rick. *Sizzle!: A Book About Heat Waves*. Minneapolis: Picture Window Books, 2005.

Explore the Web

Weather Wiz Kids: Temperature http://www.weatherwizkids.com/temperature.htm

Make Your Own Weather Station http://sln.fi.edu/weather/todo/

NASA Kids' Earth Science http://kids.mtpe.hq.nasa.gov/